WORKBOOK

For

The Invisible Ache

Black Men Identifying Their Pain and Reclaiming Their Power

An Implementation Guide to Courtney B. Vance, Dr. Robin L. Smith's Book

Stallone Publishers

Companion Workbook for [The Invisible Ache]

This companion workbook is designed to be used in conjunction with the original book, "[The Invisible Ache]," authored by [Courtney B. Vance, Dr. Robin L. Smith]. It is intended to enhance the reader's understanding of the concepts presented in the original book and provide a structured framework for exercises, activities, and reflection.

Please note that this workbook is not a standalone publication and is not intended to replace the original book. It is recommended that readers possess a copy of the original book to fully benefit from the content provided in this workbook.

Table of Contents

How to Use this Workbook 4

Summary 8

An Invitation 12

Chapter Summary 12

Key Takeaways 14

Questions for Self-Reflection 15

A Vital Tool 24

Chapter Summary 24

Key Takeaways 26

Questions for Self-Reflection 27

Where Do You Hurt? 36

Chapter Summary 36

Key Takeaways 39

Questions for Self-Reflection 40

The Only One in the Room 48

Chapter Summary 48

Key Takeaways 50

Questions for Self-Reflection 51

The Mental Health Crisis 60

Chapter Summary 60

Key Takeaways 63

Questions for Self-Reflection 65

Don't Feed the Beast..74

    Chapter Summary 74

    Key Takeaways..77

    Questions for Self-Reflection 78

The Whole Truth...88

    Chapter Summary 88

    Key Takeaways..91

    Questions for Self-Reflection 92

There's More to Life..102

    Chapter Summary 102

    Key Takeaways 105

    Questions for Self-Reflection 106

Self-Care is Nonnegotiable 112

    Chapter Summary 112

    Key Takeaways 115

    Questions for Self-Reflection 117

A New Movement, a New Momentum..................128

    Chapter Summary 128

    Key Takeaways 131

    Questions for Self-Reflection 132

Self-Evaluation Questions.................................140

How to Use this Workbook

This workbook is a companion to the book "The Invisible Ache: Black Men Identifying Their Pain and Reclaiming Their Power". It is designed to help you gain a deeper understanding of the book's key concepts, apply them to your own life, and track your personal growth journey.

Getting Started

Read the Summary of the Original Book: Before delving into the workbook, take some time to read the summary of the original book. This will provide you with a foundational understanding of the book's themes and messages.

Explore the Key Lessons for Each Chapter: Each chapter of the workbook corresponds to a chapter in the original book. For each chapter, review the key lessons and self-reflection questions.

Engage in Self-Reflection: Take the time to thoughtfully answer the self-reflection questions for each chapter. These questions will guide you in exploring your experiences, insights, and areas for personal growth.

Applying the Concepts to Your Life

Identify Actions to Take: As you work through the workbook, identify specific actions you can take to apply the concepts and strategies to your life. This could involve setting goals, developing new habits, or making changes to your state of mind.

Track Your Progress: Regularly reflect on your progress and track your accomplishments. This will help you stay motivated and recognize the positive changes you are making.

Seek Support: Don't hesitate to seek support from friends, family, or mentors as you navigate your personal growth journey. Their encouragement and guidance can be invaluable.

Utilizing the Self-Evaluation Questions

Reflect on Your Overall Journey: At the end of the workbook, take some time to answer the self-evaluation questions. These questions will help you assess your overall progress, identify areas for continued growth, and celebrate your achievements.

Gain Deeper Insights: Use the self-evaluation questions as a catalyst for deeper self-reflection. Consider journaling, creating a personal growth plan, or engaging in conversations with trusted individuals to further explore your insights.

Embrace Continuous Growth: Personal growth is a lifelong journey. Use this workbook as a starting point and continue to seek opportunities to learn, develop, and transform into the best version of yourself.

SUMMARY

The book The Invisible Ache: Black Men Identifying Their Pain and Reclaiming Their Power is a strong and informative look at the particular struggles and successes of Black men in America. The book, written by actor Courtney B. Vance and psychologist Dr. Robin L. Smith, mixes personal experiences, psychological insights, and practical techniques to help Black men recover their mental well-being and live a fulfilled life.

Vance, who has lost his father and godson to suicide, discusses his personal mental health difficulties as well as the cultural norms that frequently hinder Black males from getting treatment. He speaks frankly about the damaging preconceptions that depict Black males as tough and unemotional, and how these stereotypes may lead to feelings of isolation, shame, and suppressed emotions.

Dr. Smith, a recognized authority on Black mental health, offers a framework for comprehending the psychological elements that contribute to Black men's mental health concerns. She explores the emotional well-being of Black males as a result of historical trauma, racism, and prejudice. She also highlights the need of cultural competency in mental health care and the necessity for culturally appropriate treatment modalities.

Vance and Smith, working together, provide a comprehensive and compassionate guidance for Black males desiring to recover from their sorrow and regain their power. They provide practical ways for dealing with stress, creating resilience, and cultivating healthy relationships. They also highlight the necessity of self-care, getting professional assistance when necessary, and developing a support network of trustworthy friends and family members.

The following are some of the book's key themes:

The negative consequences of stereotypes that portray Black males as emotionless and forceful

The influence of historical trauma, racism, and prejudice on the mental health of Black males

Cultural competence is essential in mental health care.

Practical methods for dealing with stress, increasing resilience, and fostering good relationships

The significance of self-care, getting professional assistance when necessary and developing a support network

The Invisible Ache is an invaluable resource for Black males, their families, and mental health professionals interested in understanding and addressing the mental health difficulties that Black men confront in America. The book's message of optimism, perseverance, and self-empowerment is an effective antidote to the stigma associated with mental health in the Black community.

AN INVITATION

Chapter Summary

The first chapter of "The Invisible Ache: Black Men Identifying Their Pain and Reclaiming Their Power, " "An Invitation," sets the tone for the book's examination of the complicated emotional lives of Black men in America. Courtney B. Vance and Dr. Robin L. Smith, the authors, extend a warm invitation to Black males to embark on a journey of self-discovery, healing, and empowerment.

Vance, a famous actor and director, opens out about his personal issues with sorrow, bereavement, and the cultural limitations that frequently prohibit Black males from freely expressing their feelings. He describes the heartbreaking suicide deaths of his father and godson, situations that compelled him to address the deep-seated anguish and trauma that frequently goes unsaid in the Black community.

Dr. Smith, a top psychologist who specializes in Black mental health, gives a better knowledge of the psychological aspects that contribute to Black men's emotional issues. She emphasizes the influence of historical trauma, institutional racism, and microaggressions on the mental health of Black males, providing context for understanding the unseen agony that many Black men bear.

Vance and Smith craft a gripping story that challenges damaging perceptions of Black males as quiet and emotionless. They stress the significance of identifying and embracing one's sorrow, as well as understanding that vulnerability and seeking help are not marks of weakness, but rather acts of bravery and self-compassion.

The chapter finishes with an impassioned call to action, imploring Black men to accept their vulnerability, get help, and reclaim their power to heal and prosper. Vance and Smith's message of optimism and perseverance is strongly felt, serving as a guiding light for Black males navigating the intricacies of their inner lives.

Key Takeaways

Black males frequently carry an unseen aching, a deep-seated grief rooted in historical trauma, institutional racism, and cultural demands to be stoic and emotionless.

The damaging perception of Black males as unemotional and powerful stops them from openly expressing their emotions, which leads to feelings of isolation, shame, and suppressed emotions.

The first step in healing and reclaiming power is to acknowledge and accept one's grief.

Vulnerability and asking assistance are not evidence of weakness, but rather of bravery and self-compassion.

To manage the problems they experience, black males must build a support network of trustworthy friends and family members.

Maintaining mental health and well-being requires self-care.

Black males have the ability to heal and prosper, recovering their emotional well-being and leading a meaningful life.

Questions for Self-Reflection

How do you usually deal with your physical pain or discomfort?

_____

_____

_____

_____

_____

_____

_____

_____

_____

_____

_____

_____

_____

_____

_____

_____

_____

Do you have trouble identifying and acknowledging your emotions?

_____

_____

_____

_____

_____

_____

_____

_____

_____

_____

_____

_____

_____

_____

_____

_____

What are your thoughts on vulnerability?

_____

_____

_____

_____

_____

_____

_____

_____

_____

_____

_____

_____

_____

_____

_____

_____

_____

_____

Do you link vulnerability with a lack of strength?

_____

_____

_____

_____

_____

_____

_____

_____

_____

_____

_____

_____

_____

_____

_____

_____

_____

_____

_____

How can you debunk these myths and embrace vulnerability as a source of strength?

_____

_____

_____

_____

_____

_____

_____

_____

_____

_____

_____

_____

_____

_____

_____

_____

_____

What self-care routines do you currently follow?

_____

_____

_____

_____

_____

_____

_____

_____

_____

_____

_____

_____

_____

_____

_____

_____

_____

Is there anything you can do to improve your self-care?

_____

_____

_____

_____

_____

_____

_____

_____

_____

_____

_____

_____

_____

_____

_____

_____

_____

_____

How can you practice self-compassion in your daily life?

_____

_____

_____

_____

_____

_____

_____

_____

_____

_____

_____

_____

_____

_____

_____

_____

A VITAL TOOL

Chapter Summary

The chapter "A Vital Tool" in Courtney B. Vance and Dr. Robin L. Smith's book "The Invisible Ache: Black Men Identifying Their Pain and Reclaiming Their Power" highlights the significance of language in understanding and treating the emotional issues that Black men experience. According to the authors, Black males have historically been hushed and ostracized, resulting in a lack of terminology for successfully expressing their feelings. This linguistic barrier may amplify emotions of isolation, humiliation, and uncertainty, making it difficult for Black males to seek treatment and recover from their trauma.

Vance and Smith present the notion of "emotional literacy, " which they describe as the ability to recognize, comprehend, and express one's emotions in a healthy and productive way. They contend that emotional literacy is a critical ability for Black males, allowing them to manage the intricacies of their emotional life and successfully articulate their demands.

The authors offer practical ways for increasing emotional literacy, such as:

Identifying and naming emotions: Encourage Black males to become more aware of their emotional states and to identify their feelings using descriptive language.

Understanding the Roots of Emotions: Assist Black males in exploring the sources of their emotions, taking into account personal experiences, cultural influences, and societal expectations.

Emotional expression in healthy ways: Give Black males advice on how to express their feelings in acceptable and constructive ways, such as writing, talking to a trusted friend or therapist, or engaging in creative hobbies.

Vance and Smith underline that emotional literacy is not about being "emotional" or "weak;" rather, it is about being emotionally knowledgeable and self-aware. They promote emotional literacy as a tool for personal growth, empowerment, and healing among Black males.

Key Takeaways

Black males have historically been hushed and disadvantaged, resulting in a lack of terminology for successfully expressing their feelings.

This linguistic barrier may amplify emotions of isolation, humiliation, and uncertainty, making it difficult for Black males to seek treatment and recover from their trauma.

Emotional literacy is a critical asset for Black males, allowing them to manage the intricacies of their emotional life and successfully convey their demands.

Emotional literacy is recognizing and categorizing emotions, comprehending their underlying causes, and expressing emotions in healthy ways.

Emotional literacy does not imply being "emotional" or "weak;" rather, it entails being emotionally educated and self-aware.

Emotional literacy should be embraced by black males as a tool for personal growth, empowerment, and healing.

Questions for Self-Reflection

How has the historical marginalization and silence of Black males affected your mental well-being?

_____

_____

_____

_____

_____

_____

_____

_____

_____

_____

_____

_____

_____

_____

_____

_____

_____

_____

Do you have trouble putting your feelings into words?

_____

_____

_____

_____

_____

_____

_____

_____

_____

_____

_____

_____

_____

_____

_____

_____

_____

Have you ever felt alone or embarrassed as a result of your emotions?

_____

_____

_____

_____

_____

_____

_____

_____

_____

_____

_____

_____

_____

_____

_____

_____

_____

Do you consider yourself emotionally intelligent?

_____

_____

_____

_____

_____

_____

_____

_____

_____

_____

_____

_____

_____

_____

_____

_____

_____

_____

How would you characterize your ability to recognize and classify your emotions?

_____

_____

_____

_____

_____

_____

_____

_____

_____

_____

_____

_____

_____

_____

_____

_____

_____

_____

Do you comprehend what's causing your emotions?

_____

_____

_____

_____

_____

_____

_____

_____

_____

_____

_____

_____

_____

_____

_____

_____

_____

Do you think of emotional intelligence as a strength or a weakness?

_____

_____

_____

_____

_____

_____

_____

_____

_____

_____

_____

_____

_____

_____

_____

_____

_____

_____

How can you overcome any preconceived notions you may have about emotional intelligence?

_____

_____

_____

_____

_____

_____

_____

_____

_____

_____

_____

_____

_____

_____

_____

_____

_____

WHERE DO YOU HURT?

Chapter Summary

The chapter "Where Do You Hurt?" in Courtney B. Vance and Dr. Robin L. Smith's book "The Invisible Ache: Black Men Identifying Their Pain and Reclaiming Their Power" goes into the unique emotional scars that typically plague Black males. The writers recognize the special issues that Black males experience as a result of historical trauma, systematic racism, and cultural expectations, resulting in a constellation of emotional distress that can emerge in a variety of ways.

Vance and Smith investigate the influence of cultural stereotypes portraying Black males as powerful and unemotional, which leads to internalized emotion suppression and an unwillingness to seek help. They examine the notion of "masculine socialization," which frequently emphasizes the need of stoicism and emotional detachment, exacerbating Black men's emotional distress.

The authors highlight various frequent emotional scars that Black males experience, such as:

Grief and loss: Because of circumstances such as greater rates of incarceration, violence, and homicide, black males are disproportionately affected by grief and loss.

Rage and dissatisfaction: The cumulative consequences of racism, discrimination, and microaggressions on Black males can result in deep-seated rage and frustration.

Shame and guilt: Society's expectations of Black males to be tough and emotionless can lead to emotions of shame and guilt when expressing weakness or seeking help.

Worry and anxiety: For Black males, the persistent possibility of racial profiling, assault, and prejudice can add to chronic worry and anxiety.

Vance and Smith stress the need of dealing with emotional scars via self-awareness, self-compassion, and seeking help. They urge Black males to reject damaging preconnceptions and embrace their vulnerability, knowing that getting treatment is a sign of strength and self-preservation rather than weakness.

The chapter ends with a message of hope and empowerment, encouraging Black men to begin on a recovery path and reclaim their mental well-being. Vance and Smith highlight that Black males are distinguished by their perseverance, strength, and potential for healing rather than their grief.

Black males may break free from the chains of silence and shame by admitting and resolving their emotional scars, building stronger connections with themselves and others, and eventually leading a more full and genuine life.

Key Takeaways

Due to historical trauma, systematic racism, and cultural expectations, black males frequently suffer from specific emotional scars.

Emotional discomfort can be exacerbated by emotion suppression and an unwillingness to seek treatment, which are commonly founded in cultural standards and male conditioning.

Grief and loss, rage and frustration, shame and guilt, and fear and anxiety are all common emotional scars among Black males.

Addressing emotional scars via self-awareness, self-compassion, and seeking help is critical for emotional healing and reclaiming.

Breaking free from the chains of silence and shame requires challenging damaging stereotypes and embracing vulnerability.

Black men are identified by their perseverance, strength, and potential for healing, not by their grief.

Questions for Self-Reflection

How has society's expectation of Black males to be powerful and emotionless influenced your emotional well-being?

_____

_____

_____

_____

_____

_____

_____

_____

_____

_____

_____

_____

_____

_____

_____

_____

_____

_____

Have you ever felt compelled to repress your feelings or refrain from getting help because of these expectations?

_____

_____

_____

_____

_____

_____

_____

_____

_____

_____

_____

_____

_____

_____

_____

_____

_____

_____

What measures can you take to question these assumptions and accept your vulnerability?

_____

_____

_____

_____

_____

_____

_____

_____

_____

_____

_____

_____

_____

_____

_____

_____

_____

_____

_____

Which of the chapter's typical emotional scars ring true for you?

_____

_____

_____

_____

_____

_____

_____

_____

_____

_____

_____

_____

_____

_____

_____

_____

_____

_____

What effects have these emotional traumas had on your life?

_____

_____

_____

_____

_____

_____

_____

_____

_____

_____

_____

_____

_____

_____

_____

_____

_____

What methods have you tried or contemplated to heal these emotional wounds?

_____

_____

_____

_____

_____

_____

_____

_____

_____

_____

_____

_____

_____

_____

_____

_____

_____

How would you grade your self-awareness of your emotional experiences?

_____

_____

_____

_____

_____

_____

_____

_____

_____

_____

_____

_____

_____

_____

_____

_____

_____

_____

Do you treat yourself with kindness while you are dealing with your emotions?

_____

_____

_____

_____

_____

_____

_____

_____

_____

_____

_____

_____

_____

_____

_____

_____

_____

_____

THE ONLY ONE IN THE ROOM

Chapter Summary

The chapter "The Only One in the Room" in Courtney B. Vance and Dr. Robin L. Smith's book "The Invisible Ache: Black Men Identifying Their Pain and Reclaiming Their Power" delves on the isolated experiences that Black males endure in mostly white places. The writers emphasize the difficulties of being the only Black person in a space when one's identity, experiences, and viewpoints are frequently neglected or misinterpreted.

Vance and Smith explore "tokenism," which occurs when Black people are chosen or nominated to represent an entire community, frequently leading to sentiments of isolation and tokenization. They also address the microaggressions and subtle types of racism that Black males face in these contexts, which contributes to their sense of isolation.

The writers underline how these experiences have a psychological influence on Black males, leading to feelings of inadequacy, self-doubt, and a sense of not belonging. They claim that this isolation might increase emotional anguish and make it difficult for Black males to succeed in these circumstances.

Vance and Smith recommend the following tactics for managing mostly white spaces:

Creating a strong support network: Encourage Black males to engage with other Black people in order to gain mutual understanding, support, and a sense of belonging.

Increasing cultural competence: In order to be strong and resilient, emphasize the necessity of learning and respecting one's cultural identity.

Asserting one's needs assertively: Encourage Black males to stand up for themselves and advocate for their demands in a courteous and confident manner.

Breaking down prejudices and microaggressions: Make resources available for dealing with microaggressions and teaching people about damaging preconceptions.

The chapter finishes with an empowering message, pushing Black men to regain their power and prosper in any setting, no matter what problems they confront. Vance and Smith highlight that Black males are distinguished by their perseverance, strength, and distinctive contributions to society, not by their experiences of solitude.

Black males may build a feeling of belonging, cultivate self-worth, and reclaim their potential to achieve in any situation by understanding the consequences of isolation and adopting skills for navigating predominately white areas.

Key Takeaways

In predominately white areas, black males frequently experience isolation and tokenism.

These events can have a psychological influence that leads to feelings of inadequacy, self-doubt, and a sense of not belonging.

Strategies for navigating mostly white places include gaining cultural competency, assertively conveying one's needs, and fighting prejudices and microaggressions.

Black males are identified by their perseverance, tenacity, and distinctive contributions to society, not by their experiences of solitude.

Understanding the effects of isolation and establishing coping methods may assist Black males in cultivating a feeling of belonging, cultivating self-worth, and reclaiming their capacity to achieve in any context.

Questions for Self-Reflection

Have you ever felt alone or marginalized in primarily white environments?

_____

_____

_____

_____

_____

_____

_____

_____

_____

_____

_____

_____

_____

_____

_____

_____

_____

What influence have these encounters had on your feeling of belonging and self-worth?

_____

_____

_____

_____

_____

_____

_____

_____

_____

_____

_____

_____

_____

_____

_____

_____

_____

_____

What solutions have you employed to deal with the difficulties of these environments?

_____

_____

_____

_____

_____

_____

_____

_____

_____

_____

_____

_____

_____

_____

_____

_____

_____

Do you have a strong network of other Black guys or persons that can connect to your situation?

_____

_____

_____

_____

_____

_____

_____

_____

_____

_____

_____

_____

_____

_____

_____

_____

_____

_____

_____

_____

How would you describe your respect and awareness of your own cultural identity?

_____

_____

_____

_____

_____

_____

_____

_____

_____

_____

_____

_____

_____

_____

_____

_____

_____

What actions can you take to improve your cultural competency and resilience in primarily white environments?

_____

_____

_____

_____

_____

_____

_____

_____

_____

_____

_____

_____

_____

_____

_____

_____

_____

_____

Do you feel confident voicing your wants and opinions in primarily white spaces?

_____

_____

_____

_____

_____

_____

_____

_____

_____

_____

_____

_____

_____

_____

_____

_____

_____

_____

What is your usual reaction to microaggressions or damaging stereotypes?

_____

_____

_____

_____

_____

_____

_____

_____

_____

_____

_____

_____

_____

_____

_____

_____

_____

_____

THE MENTAL HEALTH CRISIS

Chapter Summary

The chapter "The Mental Health Crisis" in Courtney B. Vance and Dr. Robin L. Smith's book "The Invisible Ache: Black Men Identifying Their Pain and Reclaiming Their Power" dives at the disproportionately high prevalence of mental health difficulties encountered by Black males. The writers emphasize the intricate interaction of historical trauma, structural racism, and cultural forces that contribute to the issues.

Vance and Smith provide a striking picture of Black men's mental health inequalities, stating that they are more likely than white males to suffer from depression, anxiety, and post-traumatic stress disorder (PTSD). They also highlight the dangerously high suicide rates among Black men, particularly among young Black guys.

The writers underline the underlying roots of this mental health issue, linking it back to slavery's historical trauma, current racial discrimination, and cultural expectations of Black males to be stoic and emotionless. They contend that these circumstances have fostered a culture of quiet and emotion repression among Black males, preventing them from getting treatment and increasing their mental health problems.

Vance and Smith advocate for a holistic strategy to tackling the mental health epidemic among Black males, including the following:

Increased access to culturally competent mental health care: They advocate for more mental health services customized to Black men's unique needs and experiences, such as culturally sensitive therapists and support groups.

Addressing systemic racism and its influence on mental health: They advocate for the removal of racist structures that contribute to the mental health inequalities experienced by Black males, as well as the promotion of fairness and justice in all parts of society.

Changing social standards of masculinity: They argue for redefining masculinity to include emotional expression, vulnerability, and self-care, and they encourage Black men to get treatment without fear of stigma or criticism.

They underline the necessity of developing strong community networks and support systems where Black males feel comfortable to discuss their stories and seek help from one another.

The chapter finishes with a message of hope and resilience that encourages Black males to break the pattern of silence, seek treatment, and reclaim their emotional well-being. Vance and Smith highlight that Black males are distinguished by their strength, resilience, and ability for healing rather than their mental health difficulties.

The mental health of Black males may be addressed by acknowledging the core causes of the mental health crisis, addressing structural injustices, and encouraging culturally responsive care, resulting in happier, more satisfying lives.

Key Takeaways

Black men experience disproportionately high rates of mental health issues such as depression, anxiety, and post-traumatic stress disorder (PTSD).

Historical trauma, structural racism, and social expectations of masculinity that inhibit emotional expressiveness and vulnerability are the core causes of this mental health catastrophe.

To address the mental health crisis among Black males, a multidimensional strategy is required, which includes increasing access to culturally competent mental health care, addressing structural racism, rethinking masculinity, and encouraging community healing and support.

Black males are identified by their power, resilience, and potential for healing rather than their mental health difficulties.

Breaking the cycle of silence, getting treatment, and regaining emotional well-being are critical steps toward improving Black men's mental health.

Promoting culturally responsive treatment, eliminating institutional disparities, and establishing strong community networks are all critical steps toward creating a culture in which Black males may flourish psychologically, emotionally, and socially.

Questions for Self-Reflection

How have historical trauma, structural racism, and normative masculine norms influenced your mental health?

_____

_____

_____

_____

_____

_____

_____

_____

_____

_____

_____

_____

_____

_____

_____

_____

_____

Have you ever felt compelled to repress your feelings or refrain from getting help because of these factors?

_____

_____

_____

_____

_____

_____

_____

_____

_____

_____

_____

_____

_____

_____

_____

_____

_____

_____

_____

_____

What measures can you take to counteract these negative expectations and embrace emotional well-being?

_____

_____

_____

_____

_____

_____

_____

_____

_____

_____

_____

_____

_____

_____

_____

_____

_____

What are your current attitudes on obtaining treatment for
mental health issues?

_____

_____

_____

_____

_____

_____

_____

_____

_____

_____

_____

_____

_____

_____

_____

_____

_____

_____

Do you have any reservations about obtaining expert assistance?

_____

_____

_____

_____

_____

_____

_____

_____

_____

_____

_____

_____

_____

_____

_____

_____

How can you overcome these obstacles and prioritize your mental health?

_____

_____

_____

_____

_____

_____

_____

_____

_____

_____

_____

_____

_____

_____

_____

_____

_____

Do you have a strong network of friends, family, or mentors who can offer you emotional support?

_____

_____

_____

_____

_____

_____

_____

_____

_____

_____

_____

_____

_____

_____

_____

_____

_____

_____

How involved are you in your neighborhood?

_____

_____

_____

_____

_____

_____

_____

_____

_____

_____

_____

_____

_____

_____

_____

_____

_____

_____

How can you strengthen your bonds with other Black guys and advocate for community-based mental health initiatives?

_____

_____

_____

_____

_____

_____

_____

_____

_____

_____

_____

_____

_____

_____

_____

_____

_____

_____

_____

DON'T FEED THE BEAST

Chapter Summary

The chapter "Don't Feed the Beast" in Courtney B. Vance and Dr. Robin L. Smith's book "The Invisible Ache: Black Men Identifying Their Pain and Reclaiming Their Power" delves into the concept of self-destructive behaviors that Black men frequently use to cope with emotional pain and trauma. According to the authors, while these practices may provide short solace, they might eventually impede human growth and recovery.

Vance and Smith describe the following as prevalent self-destructive practices among Black men:

Substance abuse is defined as using alcohol, drugs, or other substances to dull emotions and escape from pain.

Avoidance and escapism: Avoiding emotional concerns by engaging in hobbies such as excessive gaming, social media use, or pornography addiction.

Risky habits include reckless driving, unprotected sex, and engagement in violence as a strategy to repress feelings and seek pleasure.

The authors underline that, while these habits may provide momentary respite, they may also lead to a vicious cycle of self-destruction, prolonging emotional misery and impeding personal progress. They suggest that these behaviors are frequently based in a lack of appropriate coping skills and an inability to handle emotions efficiently.

Vance and Smith provide ways for breaking away from self-destructive behaviors and regaining emotional control:

Encourage Black males to be more aware of their emotions, identify triggers, and recognize when they are participating in self-destructive behaviors.

Promoting the use of good coping techniques such as exercise, journaling, mindfulness practices, and seeking help from friends, family, or mental health experts.

Addressing underlying issues: Encourage Black males to seek therapy, support groups, or community-based efforts to address the underlying causes of their emotional anguish, such as historical trauma, systematic racism, and cultural constraints.

The chapter finishes with an empowering message that encourages Black males to break the cycle of self-destruction and recover their power. Vance and Smith stress the power and endurance of Black males in overcoming self-destructive behaviors and healing from emotional anguish.

Black males may break free from the shackles of self-destruction and begin on a road of healing, personal growth, and emotional well-being by gaining self-awareness, adopting healthy coping techniques, and addressing underlying issues.

Key Takeaways

As a way of coping with emotional anguish and trauma, black males frequently engage in self-destructive behaviors such as substance misuse, avoidance and escapism, and dangerous activities.

While these practices may bring brief solace, they eventually impede human growth, and healing, creating a self-destructive cycle.

Breaking away from damaging behaviors necessitates self-awareness, the development of healthy coping skills, and the resolution of underlying difficulties.

Black guys have the ability to overcome self-destructive behaviors and heal from emotional distress.

Self-awareness, healthy coping skills, and addressing underlying issues are critical for breaking free from the bonds of self-destruction and going on a path of healing, personal growth, and emotional well-being.

Questions for Self-Reflection

What are your usual coping strategies for dealing with emotional pain and stress?

_____

_____

_____

_____

_____

_____

_____

_____

_____

_____

_____

_____

_____

_____

_____

_____

_____

_____

Have you ever thought about if any of your coping techniques can be self-destructive or damaging in the long run?

_____

_____

_____

_____

_____

_____

_____

_____

_____

_____

_____

_____

_____

_____

_____

_____

_____

What measures can you take to establish more healthy and effective coping mechanisms?

_____

_____

_____

_____

_____

_____

_____

_____

_____

_____

_____

_____

_____

_____

_____

_____

_____

Can you think of any specific triggers or events that cause you to indulge in self-destructive behavior?

_____

_____

_____

_____

_____

_____

_____

_____

_____

_____

_____

_____

_____

_____

_____

_____

_____

Have you looked into the root causes of your emotional distress, such as past trauma, institutional racism, or cultural pressures?

_____

_____

_____

_____

_____

_____

_____

_____

_____

_____

_____

_____

_____

_____

_____

_____

_____

_____

What services or support systems are available to assist you in addressing the underlying causes of your emotional pain?

_____

_____

_____

_____

_____

_____

_____

_____

_____

_____

_____

_____

_____

_____

_____

_____

_____

Are you willing to make a concerted attempt to break away from self-destructive habits?

What concrete measures can you take to begin incorporating healthy coping techniques into your life?

_____

_____

_____

_____

_____

_____

_____

_____

_____

_____

_____

_____

_____

_____

_____

_____

_____

_____

What type of aid from friends, family, or experts do you require to break away from self-destructive behaviors?

_____

_____

_____

_____

_____

_____

_____

_____

_____

_____

_____

_____

_____

_____

_____

_____

_____

_____

THE WHOLE TRUTH

Chapter Summary

The chapter "The Whole Truth" from Courtney B. Vance and Dr. Robin L. Smith's book "The Invisible Ache: Black Men Identifying Their Pain and Reclaiming Their Power" serves as a powerful conclusion to the book, emphasizing the importance of embracing the totality of one's experiences, both positive and negative, to achieve true healing and empowerment.

According to the writers, Black males are frequently pushed to compartmentalize their emotions, repressing their anguish and vulnerability while creating an appearance of strength and resilience. They argue that their rejection of their own humanity has hampered their capacity to recover and restore their strength.

Vance and Smith encourage Black males to embrace the "whole truth" of their lives, admitting their anguish as well as their strengths, their problems as well as their victories. They say that an all-encompassing approach is necessary for personal growth and transformation.

The authors present a framework for accepting the entire truth, highlighting the following steps:

Accept and acknowledge your feelings: Give yourself permission to feel and process your emotions without judgment or self-criticism.

Recognize the underlying reasons of your pain: Investigate the historical, social, and psychological influences that have led to your emotional difficulties.

Find healthy outlets for your emotions: Journaling, therapy, or artistic expression are all activities that help you to express your feelings productively.

Forgive yourself and others: Let go of old grudges and resentments, relieving yourself of emotional baggage.

Embrace your talents and resilience: Recognize and celebrate your tiny and large successes.

Vance and Smith highlight that accepting the entire truth does not imply wallowing on the past, but rather using one's experiences as a catalyst for personal growth and transformation. They teach Black males to see their grief as a source of strength and perseverance rather than a source of weakness.

The chapter ends with a message of hope and encouragement, pushing Black males to begin on a healing path and reclaim their power. Vance and Smith stress the ability of Black males to overcome adversity, heal from grief, and live satisfying, real lives.

Black males may break free from the shackles of silence and suppression by accepting the whole truth of their experiences, reclaiming their emotional well-being, and emerging as strong people capable of defining their own futures.

Key Takeaways

Black males are frequently pushed to compartmentalize their emotions, repressing their anguish and vulnerability while displaying a strong and resilient image.

Personal growth and healing are hampered when one denies the "whole truth" of one's experiences, including both positive and bad parts.

Accepting and accepting feelings, understanding the core causes of sorrow, expressing emotions in healthy ways, forgiving oneself and others, and celebrating strengths are all part of embracing the complete truth.

Pain must be viewed as a source of strength and resilience rather than a source of weakness for personal growth and change.

Black males have the ability to overcome obstacles, heal from trauma, and live meaningful, true lives.

To be free of the chains of silence and concealment, one must embrace the entire truth of one's experiences.

For Black males who accept the entire truth, reclaiming emotional well-being and emerging as powerful people capable of choosing their own futures is attainable.

Questions for Self-Reflection

Do you have a tendency to compartmentalize your emotions, burying your anguish while portraying a strong image?

_____

_____

_____

_____

_____

_____

_____

_____

_____

_____

_____

_____

_____

_____

_____

_____

_____

_____

_____

How has this emotional approach influenced your growth and healing?

_____

_____

_____

_____

_____

_____

_____

_____

_____

_____

_____

_____

_____

_____

_____

_____

_____

_____

What measures can you take to begin accepting the entirety of your experiences, both positive and negative?

_____

_____

_____

_____

_____

_____

_____

_____

_____

_____

_____

_____

_____

_____

_____

_____

_____

_____

Do you allow yourself to feel and process your feelings without judging or criticizing yourself?

_____

_____

_____

_____

_____

_____

_____

_____

_____

_____

_____

_____

_____

_____

_____

_____

_____

What are your normal reactions to adversity?

_____

_____

_____

_____

_____

_____

_____

_____

_____

_____

_____

_____

_____

_____

_____

_____

_____

_____

_____

What tactics can you devise for recognizing and embracing your entire spectrum of emotions?

_____

_____

_____

_____

_____

_____

_____

_____

_____

_____

_____

_____

_____

_____

_____

_____

_____

_____

Have you investigated the historical, social, and psychological issues that may have led to your emotional difficulties?

_____

_____

_____

_____

_____

_____

_____

_____

_____

_____

_____

_____

_____

_____

_____

_____

_____

_____

What discoveries have you made concerning the underlying causes of your pain?

_____

_____

_____

_____

_____

_____

_____

_____

_____

_____

_____

_____

_____

_____

_____

_____

_____

_____

How has recognizing these core reasons influenced your healing approach?

_____

_____

_____

_____

_____

_____

_____

_____

_____

_____

_____

_____

_____

_____

_____

_____

There's More to Life

Chapter Summary

The chapter "There's More to Life" in Courtney B. Vance and Dr. Robin L. Smith's book "The Invisible Ache: Black Men Identifying Their Pain and Reclaiming Their Power" serves as a beacon of hope and inspiration, encouraging Black men to break free from the shackles of pain and embrace the endless possibilities that life has to offer.

The writers recognize the difficulties and tribulations that Black males endure, as well as the structural injustices, cultural pressures, and historical traumas that have impacted their lives. They, however, refuse to allow these obstacles define Black men's narratives. Instead, they create a picture of a future in which Black men thrive, enjoying lives full of meaning, joy, and satisfaction.

Vance and Smith highlight the significance of self-discovery and personal growth, urging Black males to follow their hobbies, abilities, and goals. They contend that Black men can achieve excellence in any career they choose, and that their contributions are critical to molding a more just and equitable society.

The writers offer a road map for Black males to follow as they embark on this path of self-discovery and satisfaction, highlighting the following steps:

Establish your values and priorities: Determine the guiding principles in your life and the things that are most important to you.

Investigate your hobbies and interests: Experiment with different hobbies to see what sparks your interest and excitement.

Make a plan and set goals: Develop a strategy for accomplishing your goals by breaking down your broader aspirations into actionable actions.

Seek help and mentorship: Make contact with people who can offer advice, encouragement, and inspiration.

Accept resilience and perseverance: Expect setbacks and obstacles, but don't let them dissuade you from achieving your objectives.

Celebrate your accomplishments: Recognize and appreciate your accomplishments, no matter how minor they may appear.

Vance and Smith highlight that the road of self-discovery and satisfaction is a continual process of development and evolution rather than a straight path. They urge Black males to consider setbacks as temporary impediments rather than permanent roadblocks, and to regard problems as chances for growth.

The chapter finishes with a powerful message of affirmation and optimism, asserting that there is more to life than suffering and struggle for Black males. Vance and Smith remind Black men of their innate power, perseverance, and potential for joy, encouraging them to accept their true selves and follow their aspirations with tenacity.

Black men may break free from the shackles of pain, regain their power, and create lives filled with purpose, passion, and fulfillment by going on this path of self-discovery. Their stories of healing and victory will serve as beacons of hope for future generations.

Key Takeaways

Due to institutional injustices, cultural pressures, and historical traumas, black males suffer obstacles and problems.

Black males should be identified by their ability for greatness, perseverance, and pleasure, not by their misery.

For Black men to break free from the chains of sorrow and live lives filled with purpose and passion, they must go on a path of self-discovery and satisfaction.

Defining values and priorities, exploring interests, creating goals, seeking help, embracing resilience, and celebrating triumphs are all important aspects in this path.

Black males are born with the fortitude, resilience, and potential for joy to overcome obstacles and live fulfilled lives.

For Black men to live real and satisfying lives, they must reclaim authority and pursue their aspirations with unrelenting commitment.

Black men's stories of recovery and victory can serve as beacons of hope for future generations.

Questions for Self-Reflection

What are your primary principles, and how do they influence your life decisions?

_____

_____

_____

_____

_____

_____

_____

_____

_____

_____

_____

_____

_____

_____

_____

_____

_____

_____

How do your values match up with your present behaviors and goals?

_____

_____

_____

_____

_____

_____

_____

_____

_____

_____

_____

_____

_____

_____

_____

_____

_____

_____

What measures can you take to make sure your behaviors reflect your values?

_____

_____

_____

_____

_____

_____

_____

_____

_____

_____

_____

_____

_____

_____

_____

_____

_____

_____

_____

What hobbies or themes pique your interest and enthusiasm?

_____

_____

_____

_____

_____

_____

_____

_____

_____

_____

_____

_____

_____

_____

_____

_____

_____

Have you lately taken the opportunity to explore new passions or interests?

_____

_____

_____

_____

_____

_____

_____

_____

_____

_____

_____

_____

_____

_____

_____

_____

_____

_____

What opportunities can you make to explore your hobbies and interests further?

_____

_____

_____

_____

_____

_____

_____

_____

_____

_____

_____

_____

_____

_____

_____

_____

_____

SELF-CARE IS NONNEGOTIABLE

Chapter Summary

The chapter "Self-Care is Nonnegotiable" in Courtney B. Vance and Dr. Robin L. Smith's book "The Invisible Ache: Black Men Identifying Their Pain and Reclaiming Their Power" highlights the critical significance of self-care in Black men's overall well-being. The writers argue that self-care is neither a luxury or a sign of weakness, but rather a fundamental component of living a healthy and full life.

Vance and Smith recognize the special obstacles that Black males experience, who frequently put the needs of others before their own and are under pressure to project a sense of power and invincibility. They say that Black men's physical, mental, and emotional health would suffer as a result of this disregard of self-care.

The authors present a thorough framework for self-care that includes the following major elements:

Physical Self-Care is the practice of prioritizing appropriate sleep, good nutrition, and regular exercise in order to preserve physical health and vitality.

Engaging in activities that improve mental well-being, such as mindfulness practices, journaling, and stress management strategies, is an example of mental self-care.

Emotional Self-Care is the practice of nurturing one's emotional well-being via self-awareness, emotional expression, and seeking help when required.

Social Self-Care is the practice of cultivating strong social ties with friends, family, and support groups in order to build a sense of belonging and community.

Spiritual Self-Care is defined as the exploration and participation in spiritual practices that create a feeling of purpose, meaning, and connection to something bigger than oneself.

Vance and Smith highlight that self-care is not a one-size-fits-all strategy, and they encourage Black men to figure out what works best for them and incorporate self-care routines into their everyday life. They also discuss typical challenges to self-care, such as time limits, cultural expectations, and internalized negative attitudes, and offer ways for overcoming them.

The chapter finishes with a strong message of empowerment, stressing that self-care is an act of self-love and self-respect, not weakness. Vance and Smith encourage Black males to prioritize self-care as a must for reaching their full potential and enjoying a life of meaning, contentment, and well-being.

Black males may break away from the pattern of neglect and adopt a holistic approach to their well-being by emphasizing self-care in all of its manifestations. Self-care is no longer a luxury, but rather a requirement that allows Black men to succeed in all parts of their lives.

Key Takeaways

Self-care is neither a luxury or a sign of weakness; it is a vital component of living a healthy and full life.

Black males frequently prioritize the needs of others over their own and are under pressure to project an image of power and invincibility, which leads to a lack of self-care.

Self-care is concerned with the physical, mental, emotional, social, and spiritual elements of one's well-being.

There is no such thing as a one-size-fits-all approach to self-care; Black men should figure out what works best for them and incorporate self-care techniques into their everyday life.

Time restrictions, cultural expectations, and internalized negative ideas are all common hurdles to self-care.

Self-care is not a sign of weakness; rather, it is an expression of self-love and self-respect.

To reach their greatest potential and live a life of purpose, contentment, and well-being, Black men must prioritize self-care.

Prioritizing self-care in all of its manifestations enables Black males to break away from the cycle of neglect and adopt a holistic approach to their health.

Self-care is not a luxury for Black guys who want to succeed in all parts of their lives.

Questions for Self-Reflection

What is your current perspective on self-care? Do you consider it a necessity or a luxury?

What are your motivations for prioritizing or disregarding self-care?

_____

_____

_____

_____

_____

_____

_____

_____

_____

_____

_____

_____

_____

_____

_____

_____

_____

What effect has your approach to self-care had on your overall well-being?

_____

_____

_____

_____

_____

_____

_____

_____

_____

_____

_____

_____

_____

_____

_____

_____

_____

What parts of your physical, mental, emotional, social, and spiritual health need to be addressed?

_____

_____

_____

_____

_____

_____

_____

_____

_____

_____

_____

_____

_____

_____

_____

_____

_____

_____

_____

What self-care methods speak to you and fit your lifestyle?

_____

_____

_____

_____

_____

_____

_____

_____

_____

_____

_____

_____

_____

_____

_____

_____

_____

What steps can you take to include self-care activities into your everyday routine?

_____

_____

_____

_____

_____

_____

_____

_____

_____

_____

_____

_____

_____

_____

_____

_____

_____

What specific hurdles or obstacles do you encounter while attempting to prioritize self-care?

_____
_____
_____
_____
_____
_____
_____
_____
_____
_____
_____
_____
_____
_____
_____
_____
_____

How do you deal with time limits, cultural expectations, and internalized negative ideas that prevent you from practicing self-care?

_____

_____

_____

_____

_____

_____

_____

_____

_____

_____

_____

_____

_____

_____

_____

_____

_____

What support systems or resources can assist you in overcoming these obstacles?

_____

_____

_____

_____

_____

_____

_____

_____

_____

_____

_____

_____

_____

_____

_____

_____

_____

_____

_____

How can self-care be reframed as an act of self-love and self-respect rather than a show of weakness?

_____

_____

_____

_____

_____

_____

_____

_____

_____

_____

_____

_____

_____

_____

_____

_____

_____

_____

_____

How can you advocate for your own self-care needs while still setting limits with others?

_____

_____

_____

_____

_____

_____

_____

_____

_____

_____

_____

_____

_____

_____

_____

_____

A New Movement, a New Momentum

Chapter Summary

The chapter "A New Movement, a New Momentum" in Courtney B. Vance and Dr. Robin L. Smith's book "The Invisible Ache: Black Men Identifying Their Pain and Reclaiming Their Power" serves as a call to action, urging Black men to embrace their collective strength and launch a new movement for healing, transformation, and empowerment. The writers foresee a future in which Black males thrive rather than merely survive, establishing a society in which they are appreciated, respected, and honored for their distinctive contributions.

Vance and Smith highlight the significance of collaborative action, recognizing that the problems that Black males confront are firmly based in structural injustices and social prejudices. They claim that individual healing and transformation are insufficient to destroy these oppressive systems; systemic change requires a social movement.

The writers present the guiding ideas for this new movement:

Self-awareness and authenticity: Black males must embrace their true selves, appreciating their grief, strength, and perseverance while letting go of the cultural expectations that have defined them for far too long.

Building strong and supportive groups is critical for Black males to recover, exchange stories, and empower one another.

Empowerment and leadership: Black males must seize their authority and assume leadership roles in a variety of societal arenas, fighting stereotypes and pushing for constructive change.

Mentorship and guidance: To advise and empower future generations, black males must develop mentorship programs and support networks.

Black males must be active participants in the battle for social justice, destroying oppressive structures, and establishing a more fair society.

Vance and Smith underline that the goal of this new movement is not to blame others or seek revenge, but rather to reclaim their power, heal their communities, and shape a brighter future for all. They urge Black males to embrace their collective strength and join forces in a movement that will change their lives and the lives of future generations.

The chapter ends with a message of optimism and resolve, proclaiming that the moment for change has arrived. Vance and Smith remind Black men of their natural strength, resilience, and potential for greatness, pushing them to band together and establish a movement that will redefine what it means to be a Black man in a society that frequently wants to marginalize and belittle them.

Black males can start a new movement that will not only heal their communities but also improve the world around them by embracing collective action and embodying the concepts of self-awareness, community, empowerment, mentoring, and social justice. Their stories of recovery, success, and collaborative strength will serve as inspiration for future generations.

Key Takeaways

Individual healing and transformation are insufficient to eliminate structural disparities and social prejudices; systemic change requires a communal movement.

Black males must accept their true selves, including their anguish, power, and perseverance.

Black males must build strong and supportive networks in order to heal, exchange stories, and empower one another.

Black males must assert their authority and assume leadership roles in different aspects of society.

It is critical to establish mentoring programs and support networks in order to advise and empower future generations.

Black males must be active participants in the battle for social justice and the destruction of oppressive structures.

This new movement is not about blaming others or pursuing vengeance; rather, it is about recovering power, rebuilding communities, and imagining a better future for all.

Adopting collective action and living the concepts of self-awareness, community, empowerment, mentoring, and social justice can change the lives of Black males and future generations.

Questions for Self-Reflection

How at ease are you with being your true self, with admitting your grief, strength, and resilience?

_____

_____

_____

_____

_____

_____

_____

_____

_____

_____

_____

_____

_____

_____

_____

_____

_____

_____

What measures can you take to increase your self-awareness and let go of society expectations that may be impeding your true expression?

_____

_____

_____

_____

_____

_____

_____

_____

_____

_____

_____

_____

_____

_____

_____

_____

_____

Do you have the confidence to take on leadership responsibilities and advocate for change?

_____

_____

_____

_____

_____

_____

_____

_____

_____

_____

_____

_____

_____

_____

_____

_____

_____

_____

What are your areas of skill or passion that you can use to help others and effect positive change?

_____

_____

_____

_____

_____

_____

_____

_____

_____

_____

_____

_____

_____

_____

_____

_____

_____

Are you actively mentoring or guiding the next generation of Black men?

_____

_____

_____

_____

_____

_____

_____

_____

_____

_____

_____

_____

_____

_____

_____

_____

What measures may you take to become a mentor or seek mentoring from seasoned professionals?

_____

_____

_____

_____

_____

_____

_____

_____

_____

_____

_____

_____

_____

_____

_____

_____

_____

How can you offer your knowledge, experiences, and insights to empower and encourage the next generation of genealogists?

_____

_____

_____

_____

_____

_____

_____

_____

_____

_____

_____

_____

_____

_____

_____

_____

_____

_____

Are you actively participating in initiatives or activities that promote social justice and oppose oppressive systems?

_____

_____

_____

_____

_____

_____

_____

_____

_____

_____

_____

_____

_____

_____

_____

_____

_____

SELF-EVALUATION QUESTIONS

1. Consider your overall development since the start of this workbook. What places have witnessed the most development? What areas still require improvement?

_____

_____

_____

_____

_____

_____

_____

_____

_____

_____

_____

_____

_____

_____

_____

_____

_____

_____

2. Recognize any patterns or themes that have formed during your self-reflection exercises. What discoveries have you made about yourself and your personal development journey?

_____

_____

_____

_____

_____

_____

_____

_____

_____

_____

_____

_____

_____

_____

_____

_____

_____

3. Assess your dedication to self-discovery and personal improvement. What difference has this workbook made in your drive and attitude to self-improvement?

_____

_____

_____

_____

_____

_____

_____

_____

_____

_____

_____

_____

_____

_____

_____

_____

_____

_____

_____

4. Evaluate your ability to apply the concepts and tactics covered in this workbook to real-world circumstances. How well have you implemented these concepts in your daily life?

_____

_____

_____

_____

_____

_____

_____

_____

_____

_____

_____

_____

_____

_____

_____

_____

_____

_____

5. Consider your support system and the part it has played in your personal development path. How have your interactions with others affected your self-awareness and growth?

_____

_____

_____

_____

_____

_____

_____

_____

_____

_____

_____

_____

_____

_____

_____

_____

_____

_____

_____

_____

6. Consider the influence of external elements on your self-perception and progress, such as society expectations, cultural standards, and personal experiences. How have you dealt with these influences?

_____

_____

_____

_____

_____

_____

_____

_____

_____

_____

_____

_____

_____

_____

_____

_____

_____

7. Assess your capacity to make specific and attainable objectives for yourself. How well have you broken down big goals into manageable chunks and monitored your progress?

_____

_____

_____

_____

_____

_____

_____

_____

_____

_____

_____

_____

_____

_____

_____

_____

_____

_____

8. Evaluate your resilience and capacity to recover from failures and adversities. How have you created tactics for dealing with misfortune while remaining optimistic?

_____

_____

_____

_____

_____

_____

_____

_____

_____

_____

_____

_____

_____

_____

_____

_____

_____

9. Consider your potential for self-compassion and acceptance. How have you developed a feeling of self-worth by learning to appreciate your flaws and strengths?

_____

_____

_____

_____

_____

_____

_____

_____

_____

_____

_____

_____

_____

_____

_____

_____

_____

_____

10. Visualize yourself in the future and the goals you want to reach. How will the insights and abilities learned from this workbook help you achieve your personal and professional goals?

_____

_____

_____

_____

_____

_____

_____

_____

_____

_____

_____

_____

_____

_____

_____

_____

Made in the USA
Monee, IL
07 November 2024

69598712R00085